M000115252

Mindset Moments

Cursive Writing
Practice

 Newmark Learning • 145 Huguenot Street • New Rochelle, NY • 10801

ISBN 978-1-4788-6134-8   Printed in Dongguan, China. 8557/0919/16266
For ordering information, call Toll-Free 1-877-279-8388 or visit our website at www.newmarklearning.com.

Table of Contents

Practice Sheets

Introduction

Welcome to *Grades 3+: Mindset Moments Cursive Writing Practice*—the perfect resource to help kids practice their cursive writing skills using growth mindset sentences.

Many young learners struggle when they begin to write. Learning to form letters with lines, circles, and a few strokes, and then writing legible words and sentences can be challenging. However, with enough practice, perseverance and a growth mindset, students can master this skill. This book is full of meaningful sentences for kids to practice cursive writing while forming a positive growth mindset.

The 40 practice sheets in this book were developed to give children cursive writing practice and opportunities to hone their fine-motor skills using growth mindset sentences such as: "Every mistake you make is progress toward your goal," and "Reflect on your work and think how you can improve."

How to Use This Book

You can use this book in a variety of ways. Here are a few ideas:

- Photocopy and distribute the Uppercase and Lowercase Letter Formation Practice pages for each child to keep at their desk. Students can reference these pages as they write their sentences.

- Before distributing the practice sheets to your students, write the growth mindset sentence on the board and model standard cursive letter formation.

- Generate rich discussions about growth mindset traits by introducing each sentence to the class. You may start by sharing what the sentence means and why it is meaningful.

- Challenge students to complete a practice sheet when they arrive in the morning.

- Invite partners or small groups to share and discuss their written sentences.

- Laminate the practice sheets and keep them in a writing center for students to complete independently with a dry erase pen. You can also keep laminated copies of the letter formation pages for children to reference as they write.

- Send home a practice sheet each night for students to complete independently or with the help of a parent, guardian, or older sibling.

- Provide copies of the blank sheet on page 48 for additional practice.

How to Use the Practice Sheets

Each practice sheet, designed to help students develop their writing skills, is comprised of four parts:

1 Trace the sentence. In this section, students trace a growth mindset sentence with the aid of dotted letters. The initial words on the first 26 pages are in alphabetical order to offer children practice with all upper- and lowercase letters. Note: You can have students complete the practice sheets in any order you choose, especially if they are having difficulty with a particular letter or group of letters.

2 Practice writing these words. Next, children write two key words from the growth mindset sentence without the aid of dotted letters. They can practice writing each word as many times as space allows.

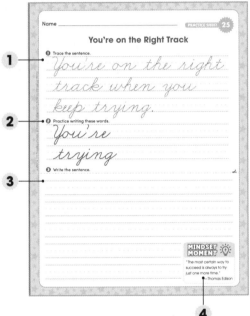

3 Write the sentence. In this section, children write the growth mindset sentence on the write-on lines provided. Encourage children to analyze their writing and focus on four areas: letter formation, sizing of letters, line alignment, and spacing between letters and words.

4 Mindset Moment. At the bottom of each sheet is a Mindset Moment box with a fun fact, growth mindset strategy, or quote that correlates to the practice sentence. After the children write their sentences, they can cut the pages on the dotted line to create their own Growth Mindset Moment book. For instructions on how to make the booklet, see page 47.

Uppercase Letter Formation Practice

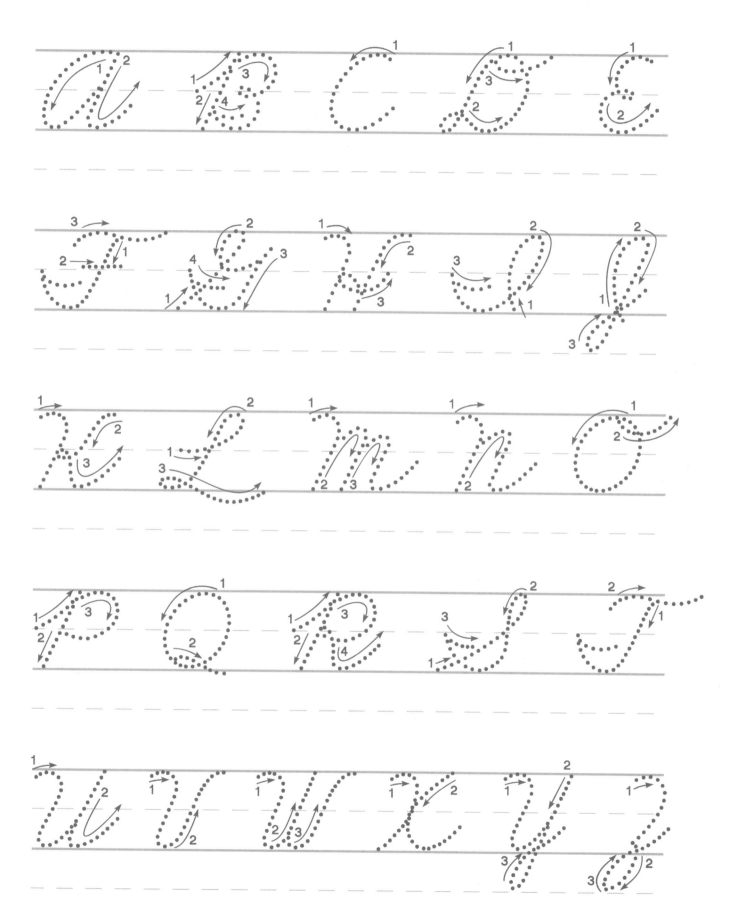

Lowercase Letter Formation Practice

Always Say "I'll Try"

1 Trace the sentence.

Always say "I'll try." Never say "I can't."

2 Practice writing these words.

Always

try

3 Write the sentence.

Grades 3+ Mindset Moments Cursive Writing Practice © Newmark Learning, LLC • page 7

MINDSET MOMENT

"If you can dream it, you can do it!"

—Walt Disney

Based on What You Know

1 Trace the sentence.

*Based on what you
already know, what
is your next step?*

2 Practice writing these words.

Based

already

3 Write the sentence.

Grades 3+ Mindset Moments Cursive Writing Practice © Newmark Learning, LLC • page 8

MINDSET MOMENT

If you can't figure out a solution for your problem, try making a list or working backwards.

Choose a Partner

1 Trace the sentence.

Choose a partner you think you can work well with.

2 Practice writing these words.

Choose

think

3 Write the sentence.

Grades 3+: Mindset Moments Cursive Writing Practice © Newmark Learning, LLC • page 9

MINDSET MOMENT

Working with a friend can be fun and productive if you both remain focused on your goals.

Don't Let Failure Be an Ending

1 Trace the sentence.

Don't let failure be an ending; let it be a beginning.

2 Practice writing these words.

Don't

ending

3 Write the sentence.

Grades 3+ Mindset Moments Cursive Writing Practice © Newmark Learning, LLC • page 10

MINDSET MOMENT

It can take several tries before you become good at something. Giving up is never an option!

Every Mistake

1 Trace the sentence.

Every mistake you make is progress toward your goal.

2 Practice writing these words.

Every

mistake

3 Write the sentence.

Grades 3+: Mindset Moments Cursive Writing Practice © Newmark Learning, LLC • page 11

MINDSET MOMENT

"A person who never made a mistake never tried anything new."
—Albert Einstein

Name _____

Failure Is When You Give Up

1 Trace the sentence.

Failure is when you give up. Until then, it's learning.

2 Practice writing these words.

Failure

then

3 Write the sentence.

Grades 3+: Mindset Moments Cursive Writing Practice © Newmark Learning, LLC • page 12

MINDSET MOMENT

"If you quit ONCE it becomes a habit. Never quit!"
—Michael Jordan

Name _____

Group Conversations

1 Trace the sentence.

Group conversations can help you find solutions.

2 Practice writing these words.

Group

solutions

3 Write the sentence.

Grades 3+: Mindset Moments Cursive Writing Practice © Newmark Learning, LLC • page 13

MINDSET MOMENT

Working in a group can help you achieve your goal and finish your task faster than working alone.

What You Learned

1 Trace the sentence.

Hour can what you learned today help you in the future?

2 Practice writing these words.

Hour

learned

3 Write the sentence.

Grades 3+: Mindset Moments Cursive Writing Practice © Newmark Learning, LLC • page 14

MINDSET MOMENT

Before you can learn cursive writing, you have to learn the alphabet and how to spell words!

Name _____

I Should Share My Ideas

1 Trace the sentence.

I should share my ideas, so others can learn from me.

2 Practice writing these words.

should

others

3 Write the sentence.

MINDSET MOMENT

Sharing ideas can lead to newer, greater ideas that might make yours even better. Try it out!

Joining a Group Talk

1 Trace the sentence.

Joining a group
talk can help you
find a new strategy.

2 Practice writing these words.

joining

strategy

3 Write the sentence.

Grades 3+ Mindset Moments Cursive Writing Practice © Newmark Learning, LLC • page 16

MINDSET MOMENT

Listening to the thoughts of others can help you gain a fresh perspective toward new solutions.

Name _____

Multiple Ways

1 Trace the sentence.

Know that there are always multiple ways to try.

2 Practice writing these words.

Know

always

3 Write the sentence.

Grades 3+: Mindset Moments Cursive Writing Practice © Newmark Learning, LLC • page 17

MINDSET MOMENT

If you can't solve a problem one way, try a different approach you haven't tried yet.

Learn From Others

1 Trace the sentence.

Listen to the ideas of others and try to learn from them.

2 Practice writing these words.

Listen

ideas

3 Write the sentence.

✂

MINDSET MOMENT

All doctors, scientists, and teachers were students once. They had to learn from others—just like you!

Name _____

Make an Effort

1 Trace the sentence.

Make an effort to speak up when working in groups.

2 Practice writing these words.

Make

effort

3 Write the sentence.

Grades 3+: Mindset Moments Cursive Writing Practice © Newmark Learning, LLC • page 19

MINDSET MOMENT

Always have at least one question or opinion prepared to share in a group discussion.

Notice Which Strategies Work

1 Trace the sentence.

Notice which strategies work for you.

2 Practice writing these words.

Notice which

3 Write the sentence.

Grades 3+: Mindset Moments Cursive Writing Practice © Newmark Learning, LLC • page 20

MINDSET MOMENT

Drawing a picture when solving a math word problem is always a good strategy. Try it!

Name _____

Open Your Mind

1 Trace the sentence.

Open your mind and read a good book or magazine.

2 Practice writing these words.

Open

magazine

3 Write the sentence.

Grades 3+: Mindset Moments Cursive Writing Practice © Newmark Learning, LLC • page 21

MINDSET MOMENT

Read as much as you can—even comic books and graphic novels! This will help your vocabulary.

Plan Your Strategy

1 Trace the sentence.

Plan your strategy

before you start

your work.

2 Practice writing these words.

Plan

your

3 Write the sentence.

Grades 3+: Mindset Moments Cursive Writing Practice © Newmark Learning, LLC • page 22

MINDSET MOMENT

Identify objectives and set goals before you start a problem. This will help you with your course of action.

Questions That Get Us Thinking

1 Trace the sentence.

Questions that get us thinking help clarify our ideas.

2 Practice writing these words.

Questions

clarify

3 Write the sentence.

Grades 3+: Mindset Moments Cursive Writing Practice © Newmark Learning, LLC • page 23

MINDSET MOMENT

Asking questions is a good way to help make something you don't fully understand clear.

Reflect on Your Work

1 Trace the sentence.

Reflect on your work
and think about how
you can improve it.

2 Practice writing these words.

Reflect

work

3 Write the sentence.

Grades 3+: Mindset Moments Cursive Writing Practice © Newmark Learning, LLC • page 24

MINDSET MOMENT

Ask the following: What did work, and what did not? What was missing? How can I make it better?

So You Made a Mistake

1 Trace the sentence.

So you made a mistake. Try something else!

2 Practice writing these words.

mistake

something

3 Write the sentence.

Grades 3+: Mindset Moments Cursive Writing Practice © Newmark Learning, LLC • page 25

MINDSET MOMENT

Mistakes are the stepping stones to learning. Every one you make is progress toward your goal.

Think Like a Scientist

1 Trace the sentence.

Think about the ways in which you acted like a scientist.

2 Practice writing these words.

Think

scientist

3 Write the sentence.

Grades 3+: Mindset Moments Cursive Writing Practice © Newmark Learning, LLC • page 26

MINDSET MOMENT

Scientists identify objectives, set goals, and gather data when working on solutions to a problem.

Name _____

Understanding a New Idea

1 Trace the sentence.

Understanding a new idea can be a challenge.

2 Practice writing these words.

Understand

challenge

3 Write the sentence.

Grades 3+: Mindset Moments Cursive Writing Practice © Newmark Learning, LLC • page 27

MINDSET MOMENT

New ideas can be difficult to grasp at first; that's why practice is so helpful toward understanding.

Value Your Mistakes

1 Trace the sentence.

Value your mistakes and learn from them. You'll get it.

2 Practice writing these words.

Value

mistakes

3 Write the sentence.

Grades 3+: Mindset Moments Cursive Writing Practice © Newmark Learning, LLC • page 28

MINDSET MOMENT

Trying different ways of doing things might reveal a faster and better way to solve a problem.

When I Try a New Strategy

1 Trace the sentence.

When I try a new strategy, I improve significantly.

2 Practice writing these words.

When

improve

3 Write the sentence.

MINDSET MOMENT

It is good to always ask yourself: What strategy am I going to try now, and what will I do to improve?

X Out Any Doubt

1 Trace the sentence.

X out any feelings of doubt. You can do it! Try again.

2 Practice writing these words.

X out

doubt

3 Write the sentence.

Grades 3+: Mindset Moments Cursive Writing Practice © Newmark Learning, LLC • page 30

MINDSET MOMENT

If you're frustrated by a task, ask a partner for help. Together, come up with new solutions.

You're on the Right Track

1 Trace the sentence.

You're on the right track when you keep trying.

2 Practice writing these words.

You're

trying

3 Write the sentence.

Grades 3+: Mindset Moments Cursive Writing Practice © Newmark Learning, LLC • page 31

MINDSET MOMENT

"The most certain way to succeed is always to try just one more time."
—Thomas Edison

Zooming to Finish First

1 Trace the sentence.

Zooming to finish first does not make your work the best.

2 Practice writing these words.

Zooming

finish

3 Write the sentence.

Grades 3+ Mindset Moments Cursive Writing Practice © Newmark Learning, LLC • page 32

MINDSET MOMENT

Ask yourself, "How can I improve my work? Am I proud to hand this in?" Quality work takes time!

Before a Discussion

1 Trace the sentence.

Before a discussion, think of how you might contribute.

2 Practice writing these words.

Before

contribute

3 Write the sentence.

Grades 3+ Mindset Moments Cursive Writing Practice © Newmark Learning, LLC • page 33

MINDSET MOMENT

Always participate and share your ideas and knowledge. You help others when you do.

Focus and Try Again

1 Trace the sentence.

Focus on the part that was difficult and try again.

2 Practice writing these words.

Focus

difficult

3 Write the sentence.

✂

MINDSET MOMENT

"I like to use the hard times in the past to motivate me today."

—Dwayne Johnson

A Challenge Is an Opportunity

1 Trace the sentence.

A challenge is really an opportunity for self growth.

2 Practice writing these words.

challenge

growth

3 Write the sentence.

Grades 3+: Mindset Moments Cursive Writing Practice © Newmark Learning, LLC • page 35

MINDSET MOMENT

Always challenge yourself with learning something new. That is how we grow and become better!

Name _____

If at First...

1 Trace the sentence.

If at first you don't succeed... you're normal!

2 Practice writing these words.

succeed

normal

3 Write the sentence.

Grades 3+: Mindset Moments Cursive Writing Practice © Newmark Learning, LLC • page 36

MINDSET MOMENT

When you don't get it right the first time, review your goal and your steps—then try again!

Successful People

❶ Trace the sentence.

Successful people are
not gifted; they just
keep trying.

❷ Practice writing these words.

Successful

gifted

❸ Write the sentence.

Grades 3+ Mindset Moments Cursive Writing Practice © Newmark Learning, LLC • page 37

MINDSET MOMENT

"It's not that I'm so smart; it's that I stay with problems longer."
—Albert Einstein

Smart Is Something You Become

1 Trace the sentence.

Smart is something you become, not something you are.

2 Practice writing these words.

Smart

become

3 Write the sentence.

Grades 3+ Mindset Moments Cursive Writing Practice © Newmark Learning, LLC • page 38

MINDSET MOMENT

"It is not always people who start out the smartest who end up the smartest."
—Carol Dweck

You Are Capable

❶ Trace the sentence.

You are capable of so much more than you can imagine.

❷ Practice writing these words.

capable

imagine

❸ Write the sentence.

MINDSET MOMENT

Remember that you are always capable of so much greatness, but it will take grit and practice.

It Is Okay to Take Risks

1 Trace the sentence.

It is okay to take risks; that is how we learn.

2 Practice writing these words.

okay

risks

3 Write the sentence.

✂

Grades 3+: Mindset Moments Cursive Writing Practice © Newmark Learning, LLC • page 40

MINDSET MOMENT

Taking risks and making mistakes are both ways to help you learn something new.

Learning Isn't Easy

1 Trace the sentence.

Learning isn't easy.

Embrace struggle

and grow.

2 Practice writing these words.

Embrace

struggle

3 Write the sentence.

Grades 3+ Mindset Moments Cursive Writing Practice © Newmark Learning, LLC • page 41

MINDSET MOMENT

"I am always doing what I cannot do yet, in order to learn how to do it."
—Vincent Van Gogh

Name _____

Practice Over and Over

1 Trace the sentence.

Practice over and

over when learning

a new subject.

2 Practice writing these words.

Practice

subject

3 Write the sentence.

✂

Grades 3+: Mindset Moments Cursive Writing Practice © Newmark Learning, LLC • page 42

MINDSET MOMENT 💡

"Don't practice until you get it right. Practice until you can't get it wrong."
—Unknown

Name _____

PRACTICE SHEET **37**

Appreciate Others

1 Trace the sentence.

*Appreciate the efforts
made by others who
help you.*

2 Practice writing these words.

*Appreciate
efforts*

3 Write the sentence.

MINDSET MOMENT

Remember to say "thank you" to anyone who helped you figure out a tough problem.

Grades 3+: Mindset Moments Cursive Writing Practice © Newmark Learning, LLC • page 43

It's Okay to Not Know

1 Trace the sentence.

It's okay to not know; it's not okay to not try.

2 Practice writing these words.

It's

know

3 Write the sentence.

Grades 3+ Mindset Moments Cursive Writing Practice © Newmark Learning, LLC • page 44

MINDSET MOMENT

"I can accept failure. Everyone fails... I can't accept not trying."
—Michael Jordan

Name _____

Ask Questions

1 Trace the sentence.

Ask questions in class to help you understand.

2 Practice writing these words.

questions

help

3 Write the sentence.

Grades 3+: Mindset Moments Cursive Writing Practice © Newmark Learning, LLC • page 45

MINDSET MOMENT

Discussing your problem with classmates can sometimes help you find the solution.

If I Work Hard

1 Trace the sentence.

If I work hard, I can learn to do anything.

2 Practice writing these words.

work

hard

3 Write the sentence.

MINDSET MOMENT

"Today is your day! Your mountain is waiting, so... Get on your way!"
—Dr. Seuss

How to Make a Growth Mindset Moment Booklet

1 After students finish writing their sentences, ask them to cut the pages along the dotted lines, discarding the top portion.

2 Make photocopies of the booklet cover at the bottom of this page and distribute them. Ask children to place the booklet cover on top of the pages, stacked in any order they choose. Optional: They can color the booklet cover and the interior pages.

3 Staple the booklet pages along the left-hand side.

Booklet Cover

My Growth Mindset Moment Book

Written by

_____

- -

_____

Grades 3+: Mindset Moments Cursive Writing Practice © Newmark Learning, LLC • page 48